I0813459

Slant Room

SLANT Room

Michael Eden Reynolds

The Porcupine's Quill

Library and Archives Canada Cataloguing in Publication

Reynolds, Michael Eden, 1973–
Slant room / by Michael Eden Reynolds.

ISBN 978-0-88984-322-6

I. Title.

PS8635.E9455S53 2009 C811'.6 C2009-903846-3

1 2 3 • 11 10 09

Published by The Porcupine's Quill, 68 Main Street, PO Box 160, Erin, Ontario NOB 1TO. http://porcupinesquill.ca

Readied for the Press by Wayne Clifford.

Represented in Canada by the Literary Press Group.
Trade orders are available from University of Toronto Press.

We acknowledge the support of the Ontario Arts Council and the Canada Council for the Arts for our publishing program. The financial support of the Government of Canada through the Book Publishing Industry Development Program is also gratefully acknowledged. Thanks, also, to the Government of Ontario through the Ontario Media Development Corporation's Ontario Book Initiative.

Table of Contents

Jenny, Syth, Rue

The lake before you is
a trap of sound –
the mist and its clinging echo
            Skeletons of word
bristle the shallows   sculpt the vapours

A frame of wind
stands stilted in the fog

begins

            to lean

SPARE Room

Spring Night in Caledon

Spring comes up like an onion,
green from its winter heart.
Sharp scent carried on a whiff of dung.

It's the night before garbage day,
warm wind stirring the frogs
into song, the highway noise

shushed. One bag of garbage
lies gutted in the ditch. One piece of trash
clatters along the drive.

The animal is nowhere to be seen –
the smell so ripe my eyes water.
I no longer know how I saw the world yesterday.

Atlantic Rain

Late April. This room
is a crate of dry goods.

Pine floor, bedclothes, goosedown and wool.
Tumbled backward, I'm time-deep in dark bog:

a trickle of raindropped spine,
frogsong hard as glass.

Ouimet Canyon

A question yawns
the forest bedrock.

Poplar buds hover
like warm breath around the branches.

Record of time and temperature:
how many zeros will it hold?

Welcome: a room in a house anyone
may come to, a room that makes you

the way that rock was split, awed,
mouth filled with rare plants and meltwater.

Estranged

The long highway home, distance
packed tight in the trunk of the car.

For that feeling … inscribed in a book
(old gift between lovers now estranged),

Neruda's *The Sea*
and the Bells.

So landlocked
salt burns the heart of prairie.

A child's drawing:
grass   house   tree   sky.

Wind and crickets.
There's no one *born* alone.

Ache in the throat
– old rain,

a hard blue pool whipped up in the stubble
rough as the sea.

Upper Laberge

Cut yourself an aspen switch;
mosquitoes thicken the muskeg.

We catch a pike in amongst the drowned willow
at the mouth of Joe Creek; water roars behind the trees.

Rhubarb,
wild strawberry,

our palms and fingertips
stained red with the fat juice.

Today, there's so much good blood
in our mouths:

sun, our two-fisted heart,
pulls open the cloud.

White River Ashfall

A mountain heaves
and settles a stratum of ash.

This story like two winters back to back
leaves no room for forgetting:

parched snow falls
cold summer long.

Glimpse

Sight is a bird
atop the spine.

Sleep is the twittering
of the closed eye.

There comes a river of fish
caught in dream's light.

The bird spreads its wings.

Let it be a kingfisher
to carry this body of dream into memory.

Let it be a tide of swifts in the gathering dusk
to dive like stars into that black cave.

Nostalgia

Somewhere, once, deep in the woods alone my ankle
turned on a root to an exquisite bloom.

That journey's turn metastasized; I'm hidden now
across the earth, so thin my body tunes the wind.

Where you cut home
across the field, I cut in
like the grub that bolls the goldenrod.

I sleep until the pond cracks into ice,
life hardens off, we're knocked white –
our elbows high in the crooks of the birch.

Loon Loon Loon

nothing holds   breathe deep
the throat's clappers
wing into voice

hatched at the slow
precipice of land-lapped
space   an air and a thicker air   a weight

and
a weight
and a weight

surface from one body
into another   past breath's
endurance

feathers lapped like gills   water
like an echo of the body

freeshell turtle   winged otter   lunged trout

Translations of Willow

Farthest echo of first word,
spare outcropped soul,
you conceive life
from nothing.

Roots
from rock
articulate stones
sand   soil   water.

Your twisted stem sings
an epic of wind,
earth's antler
calling in her dream.

Each time a fresh tongue
sounds out the old story,
each dialect of *leaf* or *flower*
speaks white seed from wood:

Newborn and oldest thing,
open the hollow syllable of your name
                        to the wind.

Again

If you come to the edge of the escarpment
out of the damaged woods as I have done,

if we walk from true forest in a time before hope,

if you and I are the long-faced bear
and come upon this in the thaw of spring
and flags and ribbons untether at once from the streets below
and wind rises and black birds lift with the wind

and carry away the paths and the animal paths,

we must lie down again and close our eyes.

Chorus

The choir behind the mountain sings
    the leaves free from the trees.

Frost descends.

The requiem begins.

Migrations

Let's leave the earth to be; I'm asleep.
The slow sky shuts. Heaven goes on without us.

– John Thompson

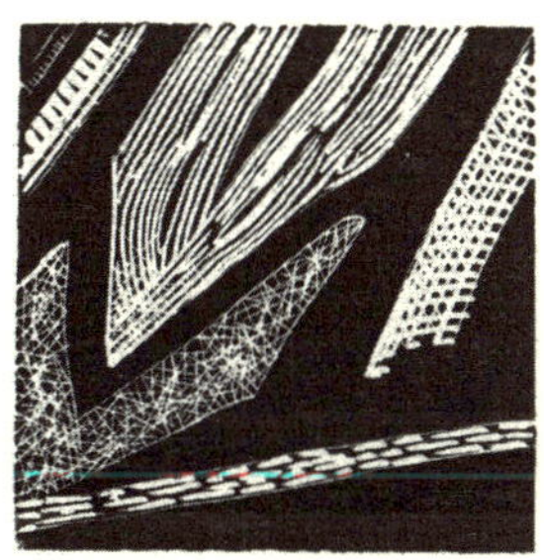

prologue
(in the voices of swans)

This is the sound of the world turning:
rough mechanism, hinge and gear.

Frost is ready to take or give.
Muscles groan, grip, slip over bone.

Sound constellates the mind.

Look up! Fix to this most distant voice.
Use this;

do not   not hear
this.

The world is not as beautiful as it was
yesterday.

Someone ringed this spruce; its trunk
weeps sap from bare flesh.

Still, animals speak: magpie
scolding   scolding.

A church, ashes framed by spruce poles, one
across the next across the next – ceiling lifted from the trees.

Beer can, survey tape, bird of prey:
we confuse the names of things.

Dye myself in aspen sap,
eat sunshine.

This is a time when a reasonable man might say
they shit, they can eat it too.

We carry this with us like ash of bone,
grey rings around our eyes: the need

to move, again begin
to live.

Beaver eats poplar shoots
all winter long.

There is a glacier. There is a meteor. There is a wind
and a great wave. There is a hole bored in heaven.

Here we go into that other beginning:
dream. Dream!

Just a dry blade of grass
between this and memory.

Stars slit the belly of summer;
there's only one *long* season in this land.

Leaping from body into body
over vast trackless space

we find our way home. Salmon
spill their luminous eggs into September.

Sky: boreal wind and light.
Hold on. Hold on.

We've landed in a body that is lost,
not even frost on whiskers,

the gnawed-down bones.

Glutted on snowberry,
food of the dead,

we begin to remember
things which haven't happened yet.

We, creators, speak: you, I,
reciprocal gods, lumps of clay, flakes of lichen.

Words fall apart. Dry husks
splay tussocks of grass.

Burn, brief star, singular rage.
Move into permafrost.

What we're doing is starving, licking
the ice knife clean.

Slow migration of absence.
Call without echo

or ear. Count the hollows. Stare hard
into wind. Stare blind. This has happened;

I've watched its reflection on the surface of a lake.
Still. Happening. Translating north across the sky.

Yes, famine. That's what I meant to tell you,
had forgotten.

As we sleep, the gee and haw of our breathing
carries us further north.

We enter each other's dream.
What do we do? Dig roots. Chew willow.

Whose eyes are these? Shiny, black-lifed
crowberry   mossberry   tonguedance.

In this dream you cross a cold river,
high water, hoofbeat on tundra.

Tell me, where am *I* now? I taste the air;
my eyelids flutter in the wind.

In one wavering cycle of breath
ice advances   retreats.

You tell me: older
than ivory tusk.

This is not wind,
it's breath of creation.

These salt tears
hold the next million years.

Hold your tongue. Rosehips
in a fold of snow. Bird's heart in winter.

What you see keeps receding, your breath
in the morning air as you shift: one side, the other.

No, you must be absolutely still or this is the end.
You are the colour of snow – but your eyes! Your tongue!

There is an argument like this: we all die,
there are no good decisions.

Will we ever again crave salt
and go down to the valley?

Is it hopeless yet?

We cover great distance
not moving. Sounds

far-reached from summer:
cicada's stung voice,

a thought's crackle in still,
dry air. At last,

is this the sound of snow, or
is this the sound that shakes the snow

like swansdown
out of winter's cloud?

SLANT Room

A snowflake, a blizzard of one, weightless, entered your room

– Mark Strand

Is the motet in operation?

– Anonymous patron

Slow Boat

A coil of water heaps the prow.
Steady-drinking, swallowless and deaf the motor drones
and slowly turns the passengers into themselves.
We're the current haul along the Mekong:
livestock jars of souvenir.

We slough our skins to water.
Twenty tongues stutter the hum of the motor:
Italian, English, Dutch, German ... a hiveful of drones
with no queen but the captain: a Laotian called Cap
whose currency's laughter and dollars and kip,
whose freightship's turned into a slapstick cruiseliner.
Nobody minds. Not a seatspring between us.
Discomfort? We paid for it.
Drinking a bit of rice whisky helps
make the riverbank slip by
more quickly –

Or slip to the roof:
the riverbank doubles.
Hover the river
stretched on a dull, beaten sheet of aluminum
drinking a quaver of kif smoke as bitter and skunky
as currant leaf. Stretched back to the ceilingless sky
there's a field winding in
that's arriving so slowly
a ball bounces into it onto the pavement beside you.
Your friends' voices rise into play
as you lie in the grass
like a riverbank under the sun.
The soundscape eddies,

plays back a tape
looped between recess bells:
You follow the pattering flow of the ball off the blacktop,
then lark a gulping somersault onto the grass. Jason

runs past and swallows the ball into play again. Dalton
and Kevin and Jeremy swallow your loop without pausing.
You save face, play dead till you drift
from the hum of the playground,
the riverbank's broad possibility wound
and verdantly bounding
and buzzing with sunlight before you –

and your name is a coil
on the tip of your tongue.

Ho Fa Hotel: On the malady of travel

This is the front desk, and behind it is your proprietor's bed. You will call him *Oldman,* or *Mr Blueshirt.*

You will give Mr Blueshirt four days in which to live this life, and in them he will never see rain.

The days are indistinct, like four ripe oranges peeled and sectioned on a white plate. You recollect them oddly: *morning, afternoon, evening, night.* Compose and recompose them: *first floor, second floor, third floor, fourth.* The hours and floors do not correspond. They are their own systems of memory.

On the morning of the first floor, Mr Blueshirt has a book in which you write – what you believe to be – your name. But it's also morning when Oldman's key sings into the padlock of door 24 and frees the pierced tongue of the latch. The door yawns.

There's a moment – standing on the second floor at the shore of this new world – when the room babbles senselessly to you. The moment before the four-legged creature barks *chair* or the sharp-winged bird whistles *fan.* The moment it takes for the far light of mountains to reach your eyes and mean *toilet* and *sink.* As you move to the bed that is already nothing like a bank of sand, you realise Oldman is gone and it's nearly dark.

At night, all the hinges lift like moths from the doors and your dreams run amok in the rooms.

On the third floor the rooms are all locked. On the fourth, the doors are boarded over. On each floor but the first, there's a balcony that looks out over the street, and in the morning the street is busy and Mr Blueshirt sits in the sun.

There are no other guests at the Ho Fa. Just two strange voices one night behind door 29. In the morning the door is ajar and the wastebasket holds orange peels and stubbed cigarettes.

In the afternoon, beyond the locked door of room 36, there's a commotion of birds. Through a crack you see flutters of shadow in sunlight.

The fourth day is a final balcony. Sun rising, or setting on the town. You are perched on the rail in the burning light. Two short hops and you burst into flight.

The Safety Pin

Beneath the autumn canopy of aspen
an endless round of ones and zeros flickers
past me – the shuttered verse of light
mid-leaffall. This is a land not yet undone
by us where *yet* springblown
will drop and multiply upon the earth.
A cog of rock, a spoke of light, the tang
of frost upon the understorey. A diapered
child toddles past. We're not quite here,
where trees are rowed in grids of old-growth.
We're swimming in the passage of a glacier,
a sheet we haven't fathomed
but are fathoming with reckless proofs.

Aleph-nought

When time at first began to slip there was,
among the extra sensitive, the sense
an extra beat sustained each act.
Where some relaxed, stretched, basked,
others cramped as if their footing spanned
a micron-width of bottomless crevasse.

By month-end it was the common talk: the lazy
second hand, the way July (so fair) had stretched
so long this year, the way even the water'd slowed
out of the taps – she laughed, *It took so long to run the bath*
I thought I'd have to put the kids to bed without.
At last I towelled them off, my watch read half of five!
I sent them out to play in their pyjamas.

A national emergency was called on August first.
A mathematician live on CNN evoking Zeno
spoke about the cardinality of fractions in a second.
A government initiative on clocks was launched: *ignore*
the sun, set forward fifteen minutes every hour, curtains
drawn by eight, but by midweek you couldn't find
two clocks alike in town. The curfew was abandoned.

Thing is, the majority are lost to this sprung time.
Kids of course do well, and many of the formerly demented.
It's certain the economy will crash,
when is difficult to pin. A handful weave between the slack
double-time intent to squirrel away the savings –
twelve bells, it's noon or midnight somewhere.

I take a walk to clear my head.
Halfway back I feel myself:
it hinges from your point of reference,
where I stand, things go on as ever.

The Microchip

step inside. We've sorted the component
parts, in turn these parts we've sorted into
their components, everything cross-referenced,
ordered to accommodate opposing
views of entropy, from everything
at once to nil and zeros and reversed.
I think you'll find it comprehensive. Though
it lacks imagination, in time and space
it is expansive – and small enough to sit
upon a pinhead. A minor glitch, the portal
does self-reference and is tough to place
in certain contexts. As such, we recommend
you always have an alternate at hand –
note my lapel pin: please, step in

There Are Many Rooms

Fall asleep. Awake and wander. The sound of creation leads you on. The lights are low, and there are no lights. The lights are all turned off. You're the only one here. There are many rooms. The doors open, or do not, and halls and stairwells make impossible connections. No one has ever been in this room before, and dust is a heavy speechlessness upon the silver hairbrush, the silver vanity and its silvered glass mirror.

You find your way in halflight, and behind you is another untouched room. You peer from a thicket of willow. The fur on your back slicks to skin and your hand falls to a banister of ringless teak.

You remember the game of hide-and-seek, and the child who believed that hiding one's eyes was fulfillment of hiding.

You wander. The sound of bamboo clacking leads you on. Even the idea of stopping is a new bloom of movement. There are many rooms, each familiar in its way.

a clean white room, and you know, when everything arrives the light will swallow itself.

You are water pushing through a house. There are many rooms. Your green hands slap the ceiling. It is

In the canyon there's a room. The sun is setting. Displayed in the corner on a rough pedestal is a detailed miniature

there are many rooms. Windows look out upon windows. Your hands are empty. You've never been here, where you draw back a curtain, step out on a balcony, keep moving

in which the rooms before you are all under construction
or being dismantled   light of all sorts is a slow heavy liquid
overtaking all around you rooms are nested into nothing

one by one the rooms go out
a white curtain
the wind catches

its nothing hem is snapped from your hand unfurling

Castor Gulo
(poem of a beaver becoming a wolverine)

This one

has teeth that grow ceaselessly in the dark
of the bank's hollow lodge   This one
scents blood packed in the far reach of winter
a bellyswell of spring kits mudpacked
warm leavening breath
scrabbles claw to ice won't rest
greenoiled dreams of sap
cycling and driving the mind's
insatiable hunger meat fat path
scratched in the arched ceiling of skull
by the calcium knit of becoming she senses them
roomed under snowpack belly taut from hours
unbroken a scab of frost
at the mouth of a winter's cache
she's come without pause or scrap
to keep the spirit housed
the edges are ragged as claws
or snapped bone sucked hollow in the bloodied snow
wrapped in mud and sticks muscle and fur to become
undone in this month of need
loosed in the hard and final air
a tear and scream unworldly fused
to beat upon the opened ground without form
swallowing whole the pulse of this being
this being becoming again in the flesh
in the belly of the lodge torn open
this being its muzzle thrust into its belly this

being this being this one

Upon the Conversion of Stephen Harper

Taking on the pallor of the poet in the thin dawn light
he stands alone from breakfast, steps outdoors
without shoes, in undershirt, cuffs of his pyjama slacks
cupped under-heel. The mountains and most distant fields
turn beneath a charge of thunderclouds. A pumpjack
in its steady thoughtless prayer is swallowed in a foam
of rain and wind-whipped flax.
                                        From the stillness
of the nearer field a riffle threads its way onto the lawn,
as if a giant wing was trailing on the earth.
The hairs upon his feet and up his legs are lifted,
his pants like tandem windsocks billow –

Inside the storm, feet bloodied on the lichen-covered rocks
and climbing, his clothes and skin translucent and alive
with light: *Sweet lord,* he cries into the broken sky,
if only you will have me, I will be true this time!

Early Spring, Canoe Lake (1917)*

It begins all white, then colour's broken light
and what you can't see: your still,
black pupil rolled back under ice.
In the foreground straight and tall, you –
Needleless Pine, roots undersnow,
underground, burrowed in the oils
and grain of the board – overtop the horizon,
hold open the picture, plot a path
between world and paint
and already a night-blue stubble of shadow
                                        gathers at your foot.
Step back – you're taking this in
with a pinpricked eclipse of an eye, the line
between earth and sky, the sweep of colour's
growth and rot. The oxidized light
on the snow tunnels a trickle of spring
into ice.
           Step forward – the near edge of thaw
tree-wells to summer, radiates
back from your trunk and you slip
the illusion we belong to ourselves. Colours draw
like water over the lip of a wading boot – you're gone.

---

* Title of a sketch painted by Tom Thomson in the spring before his death at Canoe Lake

Self-Portrait as a One-Eyed Rat (F.H. Varley, Lynn Valley, 1934)

When Varley had no relatives or friends to amuse him or be amused by him, a one-eyed rat crept out of a hole in the wall and kept him company.
– Maria Tippett

Who's there? Ah, it's you my half-blind friend.
Join me for a thimbleful of whisky. We're both
lonely for the company of the finer sex – you and I
Rat – we'll commiserate.
Come out of your hole and into my den.
There's only onions in the kitchen, and whisky –
take another capful. Tell me, what do you see
with your one eye? Me, I'm half-mad
in colour's swarm –
Hold there, Rat:
you've a good soul, but bold
asymmetry divides your face. Half, starved
a blue caved socket; the other flashes
sunlit cliff with an eye of mica. A red-gold mane
burns round you, but you're overshadowed;
its brilliance casts a pool of darkness
wherever you sit –
Rat!
I've half a mind to toss this bottle at you
but it's the last in the house
and you and I will need each other
to make it through this night.

A-frame

Hello, I announce, though this isn't quite right and I know it.
I'm in someone's backyard and don't wish to be taken
to say they're in mine: mortgaged and pinned at this ecotone's edge
ten minutes' walk by the course of a trail. The word

is just a frame of language I enter the scene through. Upstrung
ridgepole: hinge to a mudworn tarpaulin pinned open at sixty
degrees to the earth. Spruceboughs leant and packed with moss
against the blue plastic tent to make it not one. The ground

is frozen now. A split white bale of fibreglass
betrayed the shelter, drew me off the path:
white patch inside the leafless trees
before first snowfall – a plan abandoned,

left for squirrels to make
a fitful winter of, they can't resist. *Hello?*
I say again. The moss-lined bed, dull
shimmer of the zippered nylon bag a snarl

of coming from and going to. Outside,
the forest deepens, leans upon itself so every
branch and trunk becomes a doorway.

I hand myself through passages
unstopping till the evening
air gives way to snow –

once more,
Hello.

Past the fence with the ghost of the choked dog

I still hear its placeless, hoarse and beastly
pant and moan.
                    Terror beats the black pane
of my window, shapes a moose
downed by wolves in the near woods until,
rubberbooted on the hardset slush,
I stalk it to the gated streetend where I land – still blind –
in the silence of just dead.
Not till morning do I find on my return
– almost as frightening as the sound the night before –
the stiff-chained, stiff, nine-stone malamute
hung in frost against the fence.
                                        Regret
still pickets at the corner. So much we never
hope to sway with all we know, but this
I might have got a shoulder under.

Window Polishing

A sharp, four-cornered autumn afternoon upon the glass –
and through, a shadow in the lit and gritty kitchen
polishes the countertop to no effect.
A dicky-bird, advocate of evergreen

and depth, just as far from here and perched upon
a limb in both directions, protests, rebounding sharp
cubist chirps against the pane. The shadow falters, swoons
the perpendicular and leaps up plaid and fleshy

on the glass. The ladder hinged beneath
the window kilters on the grass, and flies the woozy
shadow from the kitchen trying to stop it –

          Atop the shadow, chlorophyll, ammonia and toothy

lip – preponderance of surfaces – I lift
my head obliquely from the nostrilling grass
and set it giddy, sidelong adrift the sunsponged earth.
The bird now bobbing in the surf of blades
                                        is drawing seeds out of the turf.

Left Turn

Monday afternoon
between the hours
of two and four

a lull and easy
feeling carries on
in traffic. Jack

is deeply in it. Jet-black,
steeling at the temples just
this last year, he's deep

in the routine,
full stop at the octagon,
left, right, left signal on,

release the brake and switch
to gas – left hand at two o'clock
to pull the wheel around.

The intersecting avenue
bears right of way:
a silver hatchback packed

with grade twelves on spare.
Not a cloud,
a double arch of sunlight

chromes the paint above
Jack's wheel wells,
hardens two sharp stars

that fix the black Suburban
to the moment. Two ravens
kitty-corner – both aloft,

one higher – spar
over a paper bag.
As stars spin off,

the lower bird pulls back
and pumps its wings,
escapes the brake-song's

climax, glides, a block … two …

                    a corner
          park of daycare kids,

          coats strung
          like prayer flags
          on the fence,

          the straight-eight
          swing-set chanting
          high-er! high-er!

          as the bird sails past.

Fetascope

*

Little fish, sound in the eddy of your mother's belly, your heart is clean and hollow as a stem. The world passes through you once completely while you wait.

*

Little frog, your heart is divided. Like the bend of a leg prepared to leap, the world folds back upon itself, oxbowed, every path now twice as long as every thing is twinned in thought.

*

Little turtle, you carry the world between dream and memory. Three-toned, your heart is mud and air and water.

*

Little one, yours is the four-hoofed heart that pulls itself out of the river and stands bewildered and sure. We hear you. Behind the beat of your mother's heart and mine we hear you galloping as if across a great and endless plain, and know that you will go much further than we will, and that we will slip more and more into remembering as you pass, and we pass, back through the world.

Tuesday Myth

A lesser god slips through a baffle in the air
and doesn't go back, lives out a mortal life
moment to moment, opens up a franchise shop,
wakes, works and sleeps, makes
a ceremony out of every needless meal.

Chickenpox Daughter

Snowed by bullets, it's impossible
they miss us. Our elbows hit the dirt
and snake our bodies through the grass –
a path of shaking seedheads to the trees.

We rise to our full height and stride inside
the forest, double being: owl nested
in the antlers of a stag. We walk
all night. You pluck moths
and spruce buds to sustain us, then breathe us
cross the river as we clear the trees and stride in.

On the other side we fold and curl
around a willow, the night's dream closes
like a pair of wings. In our sleep your fever
closes – your buckshot skin a Braille relief.

Soundtrack to the Moment of Your Birth

*

Already, in the first beat of the music, you are here, trilling out your present year, this month, today, the reading of this poem.

Please don't look, you'll ruin the effect. You must take a leap of faith – the dubbing is perfect. Soon you'll stand and walk across the room borne upon these words like a leaf dropped in a stream.

> your wingbeats increase, your shadow is near,
> a space before you opens, a babble,
> a furor, before you the cacophony of time.

*

The click of the latch as you step into childhood, past bedtime, awakened into your body and its nineteen months of words, and open the bedroom door to the hallway before you – rubbing your eyes just now. Just now, forever, you're rubbing your eyes toward the thin hum of the fridge somewhere far down the hall, moving into the thousand tiny handholds of dust that constellate your way, the word you're forming in your small mouth, the word with the ear at the end of the hall, the click of your tongue here at the threshold.

*

You perch at your morning window looking out across the first snowfall of your second winter as it rests, a white plane yet unbroken by the day. Not this new word *snow* that you practise, that was given by your mother with the strange light of waking, no:

it's your own wordless death come from far beyond your starlit reach to visit you
with calm;

it's the ungrown outward ring of growth that glows about the trees before you

mantled path of leafbuds leading

(all around
snow falls)

into the word of your light.

*

The dog's eternal yap agape you're strolling through a neighbourhood of crystalled June. A fence leans, one note of songbird hovers in the air and doesn't waver. A man out watering his grass is lost traversing reverie and nearly has forgotten he's a man as you stroll past the tape hiss of his stock still spray whistling a tune and catch a whiff of barbecue from down the street –

you have a standing reservation somewhere in this song,

take your time, make no decision,

stretch out beneath that bumblebee
    a spell
    and dream.

*

The bedsheet stretches out in all directions where you lie, white and cool beneath a threadcount of white sky. The autumn laundry flaps its pegging from the line.

This is someone else's dream you're in, though the rustworn tune's familiar as he carries your old bones through town – through streets your eyes have never seen. Piggyback he carries you, your tired feet dangle in their heavy leather shoes. He holds behind your knees. You hold his shoulders as he lifts a hand and points up at the church –

> this one who carries you,
> you carried – you're certain –
> along a track or cornrow once
> somewhere in the world.

*

You are here, at the heart of the great library of sounds. You rest in a simple chair and warm yourself before the fire. Your eyes are closed. Your hands are open in your lap.

It's your birthday, and outside a blizzard wails. All at once the guests arrive, push through the doors their rush of voice and laughter. The fire burns hotter as they bang off their boots, open bottles and gather round the hearth chattering, clinking glasses – and still they stream in. Snowflakes whirl and drift upon the air, mingle with the amber noise rising in the room.

In your chair, hands in your lap, eyes still closed, you're smiling – fire blazing, wind howling! Far above you windows burst and the delighted guests *oooh!* and *ahhh!* and then applaud the sound of wings and cooing – the dust of glass cascades around you.

> Beyond this nearer din you keen your ear into the vaulted attics of the library. There in the raging wind a chorus of swans moves through the storm.
>
> Far below you now, the guests have started singing.

Fugue

I heard the telephone ringing deep
Down in a blue crevasse.
I did not answer it and could
Hardly bear to pass.

– W.S. Graham

The Pond

Sunup casts a bank of pipes and bows
upon the scrim. The surface coughs and swallows
back a carp. Water, flora, muck
and methane tune from mist; frogsong starts.

Sun high now, nymphskins tinder dragonflies
rattling from sedge to pluck mosquitoes
from the air. Cicada's note crescendoes
into noon's cacophony. A bank of stormcloud
takes the sun and wind whips silver
green's canopy –

A child once saw a doe here bend to drink.

                    Cattail beats the summer
heat to death. Beaver drops the poplar
ceiling, staves the freeze; winterlong within
the vaulted room the musky hum sustains.

The Refrigerator

Ice furnace, white mammoth, airtight
purr restraining all the stars of space.
Freonated coils in figure eights
stand in preservation. Five-by-two
by two-point-five it stands.
                                        I bend, replace
the milk, push closed the door and wash my cup.
Water deep inside the glacier moves
ceaseless through its pale blue, pitched black rooms.
I pass a cloth across the countertop.

There's a constellation I compose;
door ajar its mass of starlight hums.
There's a coded starmap to behold;
I occupy a station in the field.

The hunter lays a beast in snow.

The Meat Tray

The audience lies naked in the opera
house. An earwig's ultrasound
counterpoints soprano voice, coattails
canals of human waste as contraband
placebos are traded down the aisles.

There's a bear in our midst; a terror
shadows each of us. From nightsky's reach
we pull it down on top of us, the paw
that turns the stone and pulls
our roots and tunnels to its maw.

Down the aisles an icy mist of ether
swallows us. Onstage the princess
sleeps, breasts bared awaiting ever's kiss.

A string of ears withers down the row.

The Grain of Sand

Maze of one, speck of time, winnowed
to my pocket from the wide and cloudless
night, I feel you winking blindly
at the stars in steady sequence.
Long-winded you've come to me from eye
to eye, from dunes where centuries ago
you scored hoofbeats of Mongol horses,
galeforced up across the continental strait to here.

The glacier's melt exposes siftling grit,
digestif to the grouse which eats and shits
the world in dumb perfection.
A man is lost awaiting some instruction.

Somewhere inside the ice a cellphone rings.

The Double Espresso

Star's collapse, demitasse of black,
the oil-slick moment presses through a sub-
atomic aperture. *Adagio*
to *presto,* a strange century disrobes
before I've had my toast and jam. I knock
a cup of sugar cubes, it spits across
the tabletop – metric archipelago.

Adrift a month of days the sun
can't set, I start to think it never
will again – or only once. A hiss
of hydrogen sings empty to the sky.
The table leans. A whiff of steam
escapes, turns in its ravelled seam
and vanishes, sinks a nether city.

The Coconut

A tightship freshet palmdrops seaward, sounds
and bobs, embarks to troll for foreign shores.
Landless, sunset's slick retreat congeals,
tars the ocean's gills and stills the ark's freeway.

I ring the bell again, the empty lobby
damply swallows it. A pair of snails
progress at odds across the countertop,
their inevitable intercourse a thunderclap.
The contents of my suitcase counter violently.

All night I pole my way across the tundra;
the bloody speculum of morning draws the delta.

The ocean's drift is littered as a market.

The Dandelion

Day star, tar blossom. An idling diesel,
distant, stalls the earth to stillness
in a hiccup. A seed up in the jetstream
stops mid-flight – reverses.
A phrase of song upon a failing thermal,
shaken with an apron's flour
intercepts the little star in daylight.

Far below, away, a child alone – fist
of hollow flower stems outthrust –
hears the windborne music wrinkle. A screen
of vapours closes in the sun. The basement
walls are riddled now with taproots.
Upstairs a lullaby of weekdays loops.

The child's offer settles into fossil.

The Fire Pit

The rock-toothed mouth is full of ash; handfuls
sift to bits of bone, a blade of glass,
a loop of wire. I lay them on a scrap
of cloth beside the pit – grass flat
where something's slept. The houses round
the cul-de-sac are gutted, windows smashed,
poplars suckering the yards. I drop
again into the pit, barehanded
dig the grey sleeve through
to where the platform stands.
I board a train, sit and rattle lost
along the tunnels. Across the aisle
a woman's face from out a scarf begins
to speak: *Long ago, people starve –*

The Grocery List

Half completed – half struck out: jots
to tally seventeen in foreign script,
characters with shoulders sloped, lizards,
cats and coiled shrubs all penned
to sailcloth. Beached, I found the page
salt-stiff where surf collapses rooms
of sunlight from the water. Crabs
have dragged their markings to the foliage,
and here a batt of fibreglass pulps
the jungle floor. A set of steps
recounts a path entangled with disuse.
I turn the list and shake the pathway loose.

The Radio Tower

Voices sing a spine unarched from earth.
The nervous tines of steel are lapped
like silver tongues into a net the sky
is dragged across, and one by one the minnowed
thoughts are lifted out and read aloud
to someplace else.
                                        Across the market,
flies erupt in static swarm. A merchant
hawking trays of songbirds propped
with batteries and stacks of bills and clones
of DVDs, squats and sweats beneath the sun.
Voices sing a round of news.
The village lunatic skyward sways.

I hack the jungled mountain back to mist.

The Phonograph

The tune plays on out on the terrace,
along, atop, beneath the rain that gutters
ash, chokes drainpipes, buckles sewers.
On and on the bit of glass winds pathways
round the cylinder while song unravels
from the resonator. The metre falls.
A colonnade of cedar trees is glassed,
collapses. The spindle sighs a golden
bowstring on the sleet, and in the streets
below the flow of magma slows and hardens
to obsidian. Snow falls. A grouse lights,
skating to a stop atop the terrace
and in the moment carves new space.

The snow remembers everything it covers.

The Piano

Behemoth, driven to the ice by flies,
it was the hunter drove her over. She broke
her legs; he couldn't reach her, so she languished,
crushed while cold in endless variation
through her body sounded. Sky folded.

Centuries of metronome
conduct me room by room through ice
and sediment, obsidian and ivory.
I ford a freshet toward the song but find
my passage blocked; a pane of ice
seals off the tune. I kick it into shivers.

Catacomb of living rooms: snowbear's lost
and broken prey are strewn like cities.

The Parking Meter

A rusty spring unbinds as winter's ticket
folds forgotten to a pocket. The sunlit
square flares to life. A juggler keeps
aloft a motley loop – china pig,
ukulele, Frisbees – swaps in a patron's
hat to crowd's delight. Hot dog and pop
an even five, kids throw fountain fish
their bun ends.
By stroke of three the sun
burns clear the square.
Picket-limbed
a daughter falls upon a patch of rhubarb,
turns the leaves and plugs her mouth with slugs
before she puckers in the stems.
A last carp, rogue-lung
heaving, hauls overland her bellyful,
dowses for a pool to take her eggs.

The Birthday Cake

Baked equation, iced clock. I turn
and walk my footprints back across the ice,
pick thirty-two stars out between the clouds
and nearly fall in a crevasse.
Song that sings inside the song,
cake inside the cake inside:
butter, egg, sugar, flour, a shifting
maze of poppy seed designs the batter.

The beast shrugs off its winter coat. It crumples
to the floor. A butter-coloured kid
steps out and shuffles cross-eyed
through the leaves and glass into the kitchen.
Pawprints stitch a loess of flour before the oven
– a flawless golden cake inside.

The Eyeglasses

We pass them round the village circle – a ring
of rocks around a fire. They ride along
the thin equator and flutter like a pair
of wings. Star and firelight wrap
the lenses – speech untongues
between us. We are an accidental clan,
amnesiac, an alphabet of relics
each to each. Behind the pupils' wrapping,
are we unique or sum of one?
                                                            Rain
moves off from runnelling the terraces.
Unparented, the children sucking sweet figs
wander, and the youngest with his good eye
patched returns his memory to myth.
The starlight turns its song into cicadas.

The Desk

At last she ran aground upon the garden's
feral green, her timbers split, the fug
of campfire in the air. One leg
ruddered she'd ridden out the plates' drift
and the stars'. But now another language drops
to earth between the leaves and lapses into
story. The captain's wandered off and left
no script but this shifting stanza's echo
to inhabit. Sunset steeps the pond,
frogsong done. A once-fleet stag
steps up to browse where willow splits the concrete.

The children, breathless, huddle round this end;
fire's gold mnemonic flickers. *Tell it,*
one says to the form, *tell it again.*

The Claptrap

Frog born with a frog in her throat, sacred
note withheld between horsetail and fiddlehead –
she squats, boulder-big, red and blister-skinned
by the algae pot, watches a codswallop breach
and roll back to muck. A milk-blue eruption
half clouds her one eye; the other, brilliant,
is big as an apple, yellow and keyholed
lightswallowing black.
Nearby a blowfly's hum
cuts to a figleaf, a scrabbling poppycock
spots it, pecks for a gobble but misses. Fly,
blown over the pond, now zips to the mouth
of the frog where mouths inside mouths
clap open like locks to the bluebottle dive.

Notes

The epigraph for 'Migrations' is from ghazal V of John Thompson's *Stilt Jack.*

The first epigraph for 'Slant Room' is from 'A Piece of the Storm' in Mark Strand's *Blizzard of One.*

The epigraph to 'Self Portrait as a One-Eyed Rat' is from Maria Tippett's biography of F.H. Varley, *Stormy Weather.*

The epigraph to 'Fugue' is from W.H. Graham's poem, 'Malcolm Mooney's Land'.

'The Fire Pit' was inspired in part by Mrs Dorothy Johnson of Kluane First Nation.

'Castor Gulo' owes its genesis to Lisa Guenther. The poem is for her and Rohan Quinby.

Acknowledgements

An earlier version of 'Migrations' was published as a chapbook in 2001 by Patricia Robertson's Linnaea Press.

'Translations of Willow' was the 2002 recipient of the John Haines Award for Poetry (*ICE-FLOE: International Poetry of the Far North,* AK).

'Ho Fa Hotel: On the Malady of Travel' was a winner in *Grain*'s 2002 Short Grain Contest.

'*Early Spring, Canoe Lake* (1917)' received the *Fiddlehead*'s 2005 Ralph Gustafson Poetry Prize.

'Castor Gulo (poem of a beaver becoming a wolverine)' took second place in *ARC* Magazine's 2006 Poem of the Year contest.

'Fugue' (in various incarnations) was a finalist in the 2005 CBC Literary Awards, the 2006 Bronwen Wallace Memorial Award, and the *Malahat Review*'s 2007 Long Poem Contest.

'Soundtrack to the Moment of Your Birth' was performed with music composed by Andrea McColeman at the Yukon Arts Centre for 'The Longest Night' in 2006.

'A-frame', first published in *PRISM* was selected by Stephanie Bolster for inclusion in *The Best of Canadian Poetry in English 2008* (Tightrope Books).

'Aleph-nought' and 'Upon the Conversion of Stephen Harper' won first and second place respectively in *PRISM*'s inaugural poetry contest.

Versions of several other poems were first published in some of the magazines mentioned above. A few were also published in *Out of Service* (a Whitehorse magazine whose title was, it turns out, tough to outrun). Thanks to the editors and staff of all these magazines for their support.

My thanks also to the Yukon Advanced Artist Award Program (Lotteries Yukon) for grants which bought me time to write.

I'm grateful to Morgan Whibley for the author photo, to John Steins for the cover linocut and interior wood engravings, and to each for his generous spirit.

Patricia Robertson and Erling Friis-Bastaad have been essential mentors to me. Wayne Clifford, Zach Wells, Mitch Miyagawa, Wilma Reynolds (my Mom), (Auntie) Marianne Vespry, and Jenny Charchun, have offered their ears and eyes to many of these poems and helped me make them better. Thanks to each of you. I'm especially grateful to my brother Brett who gave the whole book his full and considerable attention.

MORGAN WHIBLEY

Michael Eden Reynolds was born in Ottawa in 1973, but spent most of his childhood in Caledon, Ontario. He attended the University of Guelph before taking a summer job as a breakfast cook in Dawson City, Yukon, in 1995. He travelled in Asia in 1999 and 2000. Since completing a social work degree at Yukon College in 2003, he's worked as a supported-independent-living worker for adults with disabilities. Michael lives in Whitehorse, Yukon, with his wife Jenny and their two children.

Reynolds' poems have won the Ralph Gustafson Poetry Prize, and the John Haines Award for Poetry. He was also a finalist for the CBC Literary Awards in 2005, the Bronwen Wallace Memorial Award in 2006, and the *Malahat Review* Long Poem Contest in 2007. His work has been anthologized in *The Best of Canadian Poetry in English 2008,* edited by Molly Peacock and Stephanie Bolster (Tightrope Books).